STAR WARS

WHAT MAKES A
MONSTER?

Written by Adam Bray

LONDON, NEW YORK, MUNICH,
MELBOURNE, AND DELHI

Editor Lisa Stock
Senior Editor Sadie Smith
Managing Editor Laura Gilbert
Design Manager Maxine Pedliham
Art Director Lisa Lanzarini
Publishing Manager Julie Ferris
Publishing Director Simon Beecroft
Pre-Production Producer Marc Staples
Producer David Appleyard

DK India
Senior Editor Garima Sharma
Deputy Managing Editor Chitra Subramanyam
Assistant Art Editors Karan Chaudhary,
Pallavi Kapur
Deputy Managing Art Editor Neha Ahuja
Pre-Production Manager Sunil Sharma
DTP Designer Umesh Singh Rawat

Reading Consultant
Linda Gambrell, PhD.

For Lucasfilm
Executive Editor Jonathan W. Rinzler
Art Director Troy Alders
Manager of the Holocron Leland Chee
Director of Publishing Carol Roeder

First American Edition, 2014

13 14 15 16 10 9 8 7 6 5 4 3 2 1
001-196552-Apr/14

Published in the United States by DK Publishing
345 Hudson Street,
New York, New York 10014

Copyright © 2014 Lucasfilm Ltd. and ™
All rights reserved.
Used under authorization.

Page design © 2014 Dorling Kindersley Limited.

Published in Great Britain by
Dorling Kindersley Limited

A catalog record for this book is available
from the Library of Congress.

ISBN: 978-1-4654-1990-3 (Hardcover)
ISBN: 978-1-4654-1991-0 (Paperback)

Color reproduction by Alta Image Ltd, UK
Printed and bound in China by
South China Printing Company Ltd.

Discover more at
www.dk.com
www.starwars.com

Contents

What Are Monsters?

Throughout the galaxy there are some terrifying villains, dangerous weapons, and crooked criminals. Jedi Knights protect others from all of these evils, but lurking in the dark may be another huge threat—monsters!

These beasts travel on land, in the sea, in the sky, and even in space. Although they may threaten the Jedi and the Rebel Alliance, monsters are not naturally evil. They don't start wars or try to rule the galaxy, and they attack villains, too. Of course they can be scary and violent, but often they are just defending their way of life, or doing their job as a gangster's guard, an arena beast, or

an assassin for the Jedi's great enemy, the
Sith. Sometimes a dangerous monster can
even be trained to help the Jedi.

You are about to meet these amazing
monsters from across the galaxy. A few are
driven by savage instincts, while others
possess basic intelligence—but you can be
sure that all of them are wild at heart.

MONSTERS
OF THE GALAXY

The galaxy is made up of many different planets with varying climates and conditions. Not all planets support life, but some of the most ferocious and bizarre monsters can be found on those planets with even the harshest environments.

TATOOINE

Tatooine is a hot desert planet covered in vast sand dunes and massive rock formations.

INHABITANTS: 200,000
SURFACE WATER: 1%
MONSTERS: Bantha, massiff, Kowakian monkey-lizard, Bubo, worrt, rancor, sarlacc, Hoover, rock wart, womp rat, eopie, ronto, dewback (below)

HOTH

Hoth is a frozen world of snow fields and ice caves.

INHABITANTS: No permanent population
SURFACE WATER: 100%
MONSTERS: Wampa, tauntaun (below)

NABOO

Naboo is a lush planet with fertile lakes and seas, dense forests, and green plains.

INHABITANTS: 4.5 billion
SURFACE WATER: 85%
MONSTERS: Opee sea killer, colo claw fish, sando aqua monster, fambaa, aiwha, kaadu (below)

GEONOSIS

Geonosis is a harsh, desert planet with frequent sand storms, strong radiation, and intense heat from the sun.

INHABITANTS: 100 billion
SURFACE WATER: 5%
MONSTERS: Massiff, acklay, nexu, orray, reek (below)

FELUCIA

Felucia is a dangerous world covered in dense fungal forests.

INHABITANTS: 8.5 million
SURFACE WATER: 75%
MONSTERS: Rancor, gelagrub (below)

UTAPAU

Utapau is a planet covered in limestone formations. Cities are located in canyon-like sinkholes.

INHABITANTS: 95 million
SURFACE WATER: Less than 1%
MONSTERS: Dactillion (above), varactyl, ginntho

KASHYYYK

Kashyyyk, the Wookiee homeworld, is a jungle planet dominated by giant wroshyr trees.

INHABITANTS: 45 million
SURFACE WATER: 60%
MONSTER: Can-cell

KAMINO

Kamino is a stormy water world where all creatures have been adapted to spend at least some of their time in the sea.

INHABITANTS: 1 billion
SURFACE WATER: 100%
MONSTER: Aiwha

CORUSCANT

Coruscant is an overcrowded and polluted world covered by a vast city. Most animals are imported pests.

INHABITANTS: 1 trillion
SURFACE WATER: Only stored in artificial reservoirs
MONSTERS: Kouhun, conduit worm, duracrete slug (below)

SPACE

The atmosphere in space is a vacuum and lacks oxygen. Asteroids provide minerals, and starships supply metal and electrical parts for creatures to consume.

MONSTERS: Mynock, dianoga, giant space slug (below)

Creatures of the Deep

Many planets across the galaxy have lots of surface water. Some, such as Naboo, have water in the form of swamps, lakes, and oceans. Other planets, like Kamino, are almost completely covered by water. These waters are home to all sorts of sea creatures—some fearsome and some very strange.

Jedi Master Qui-Gon Jinn and his apprentice, Obi-Wan Kenobi, encountered gigantic sea monsters during their adventures. When they traveled from the underwater city of Otoh Gunga to the city of Theed

on Naboo in a Gungan sub, they were almost eaten by some of them!

Deep beneath the sea on Naboo lives a population of Gungans who live inside large, glowing pods. They travel in tribubble bongo subs, which look like sea creatures and have skeletons made of living coral. Traveling near the surface is usually safe, but few Gungans dare to venture deep into the watery core of the planet for fear of the great monsters lurking there.

SEA MONSTERS
OF NABOO

Naboo's lakes and seas are rich with life. The planet's waters have an ideal mix of nutrients and sunlight to support a flourishing food chain, from tiny plankton to sea monsters of the abyss.

Powerful back legs

Glowing tentacles

Tough armor plates

OPEE SEA KILLER
Length: 20 m (65 ft 7 in)
Habitat: Clings to crags in Naboo's deep lakes and seas
Notable Features: Jet propulsion vents on the body, tail legs, and extendable tongue

Multidirectional eyestalks

Webbed hands help with swimming

Long, sticky tongue

COLO CLAW FISH
Length: 40 m (131 ft 3 in)
Habitat: Sea caves
Notable Features: Venomous fangs, angling lures, and grasping claws

Luminescent skin patterns

Angling lures

"There is always a bigger fish."
Qui-Gon Jinn

Tiny eyes

SANDO AQUA MONSTER
Length: 160 m (525 ft)
Habitat: Open oceans and sea caves
Notable Features: Webbed hands, powerful tail, has both gills and lungs, and body not fully adapted for swimming

Strong jaws for powerful bite

Gills

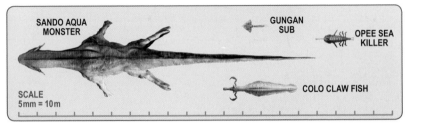

SANDO AQUA MONSTER

GUNGAN SUB

OPEE SEA KILLER

COLO CLAW FISH

SCALE
5mm = 10m

13

Deep in the waters of Naboo lurks a
ferocious hunter—the opee sea killer. The
opee is a giant fish, but it has features similar
to other kinds of creatures as well. It is
armored with heavy scales, like a crab. It
also has three pairs of legs on its tail, which
it uses to swim and perch on large rocks.

Opees are patient hunters. They wait
in the dark and use long, glowing lures
to entice their prey. Creatures that swim too
close are sucked in when the opees open their
mouths, and are then shredded by many rows

of knife-like teeth. Opees can also catch schools of fish from far away by shooting out their long, sticky tongues.

Qui-Gon, Obi-Wan, and their Gungan friend Jar Jar Binks were once attacked by an opee. It caught their sub with its tongue and nearly swallowed it! Fortunately the opee was attacked by another monster and let them go. They retreated to a cave but would soon find that they were not alone there.

Opees of all sizes are dangerous. Baby opees are attracted to the lights of Gungan cities and have been known to hunt Gungans who swim too far from home.

Baby opees must beware though—they are a favorite food for the colo claw fish, which is the second-largest sea monster on Naboo. The colo hides in limestone caves deep in the watery abyss where it waits for unsuspecting prey. Much like the opee, the colo attracts smaller monsters using glowing spots along its body. When it senses prey, the colo stuns its victims with a powerful shriek! Then the monster uses claws on both sides of its ugly face to grab and pull the prey into its

mouth, stinging it with paralyzing venom.
The colo often swallows its prey whole.
If this happens to a baby opee, it can chew
its way out of the claw fish's stomach. If the
prey is too big to swallow, the colo can also
unhinge its jaw like a snake.

The Jedi had steered their sub away from
the opee—but unknowingly straight toward
a colo claw fish. The monster was about to
grab their ship, but the colo was attacked
and eaten by an even larger sea beast!

The sando aqua monster is the largest of all of Naboo's sea beasts. Despite its size of more than 160 meters (525 feet) long, sandos are rarely seen because they blend in so well with the large boulders found in deep seas. However, Jar Jar and the unlucky Jedi met this huge beast twice on their adventurous ride under the sea. Thankfully, the sando was more interested in eating the other Naboo sea monsters than the Jedi.

Sandos have gills, webbed feet and hands, as well as a long, powerful tail with fins. This makes them very well adapted for life underwater. Other features, such as a muscular body, powerful legs, and lungs for breathing air, are usually found in land creatures. The combination of these features allows sandos to catch and eat not only opees and colos in the sea, but also land-dwelling fambaas and falumpasets. Very few creatures can escape the razor-sharp claws and teeth of this aquatic beast!

>REPORT : GUNGAN SEA

On a mission through the seas of Naboo, Jedi Qui-Gon Jinn, Obi-Wan Kenobi, and Gungan Jar Jar Binks encountered three of the worst sea monsters of the abyss. Their report follows.

REPORT LOG 1

Gungan bongo submarine, carrying two Jedi and Jar Jar Binks, attacked by opee sea killer. Immediate power loss and significant damage to the sub.

REPORT LOG 2

Engine malfunction repaired and power supply restored by Jedi Padawan Kenobi. Colo claw fish identified at close range. Crew fled the area at maximum speed.

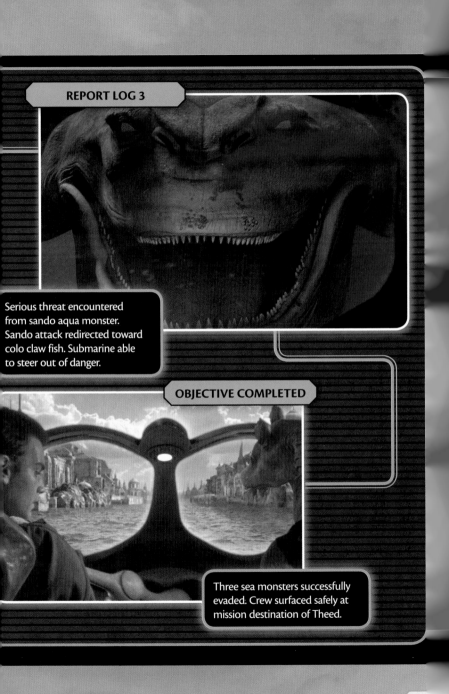

Serious threat encountered from sando aqua monster. Sando attack redirected toward colo claw fish. Submarine able to steer out of danger.

OBJECTIVE COMPLETED

Three sea monsters successfully evaded. Crew surfaced safely at mission destination of Theed.

Land Monsters

There are land monsters living on many planets. Some have adapted well to the extreme dry heat and intense sun of planets such as Tatooine and Geonosis. Others are better suited to the humid, fertile lands of Felucia or swampy Dagobah. Planets like Naboo or the moon of Endor have more comfortable environments for beasts to thrive in.

When Jedi Qui-Gon Jinn and Obi-Wan Kenobi first arrived on the planet Naboo, they saw just how diverse a planet's monsters could be. An advancing droid army scared

all of Naboo's wildlife from the forest, including the graceful ikopi, lumbering falumpasets, and little pikobis, nunas, and motts. Indeed Qui-Gon and Obi-Wan were nearly run over by the stampeding beasts!

Even frozen worlds such as Hoth are not too hostile for life to survive. Rebel Alliance soldiers discovered several kinds of creatures, including the docile tauntauns and the savage marauding wampas, while they were building Echo Base on Hoth.

LAND BEAST VS.
THE JEDI

A fight with a land beast can mean certain doom for most inhabitants of the galaxy. But the Jedi are always prepared! They do not require anything other than their wits and a lightsaber.

LIGHTSABER
Lightsabers are the primary weapons of the Jedi. They prefer these ancient laser-swords over clumsy blasters. Every lightsaber is different, as each Jedi builds his own.

THE FORCE
The Jedi draw their power from the Force. Anakin Skywalker used the Force to control a dangerous beast.

UTILITY BELT
Jedi keep utility belt equipment to a minimum. Basic supplies include breathers for underwater travel, medical supplies, tools, and energy capsules.

Medical kit

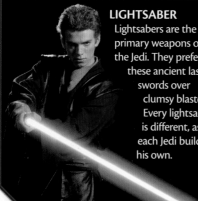

WHAT IF YOU ARE NOT A JEDI?
Padmé Amidala was not a Jedi Knight. So when she fought alongside the Jedi, she had to rely on a blaster, which may only cause temporary damage to a monster.

Blaster

Lightsaber hilt

Synthetic leather coat offers protection against attacks

Two-handed grip for full control

Blue energy blade is maneuverable and powerful enough to fight a monster

Loose-fitting tunic for freedom of movement

Practical travel boots

Trousers designed for combat

Food capsules

The ferocious wampa is the greatest predator on Hoth. Standing at 3 meters (9 feet 10 inches) tall, with razor-sharp claws and teeth, wampas are a terrifying sight for anyone who encounters them.

Luke Skywalker was attacked by an enormous wampa on Hoth. The creature dragged Luke and his tauntaun back to its cave to eat. Fortunately for Luke, the wampa ate the tauntaun first, giving Luke enough time to figure out how he could escape.

A wampa's thick, white fur not only keeps it warm, but also helps camouflage the monster when it is hunting in the snow. Wampas mostly hunt tauntauns, which they kill and bring back to their caves. They make sure not to waste any of their meat because they might not find another tauntaun for a long time. Wampas hang their prey upside down in the ice, storing it so that they and their cubs can eat it later.

ESCAPE FROM A WAMPA

In the icy wastelands of Hoth, Luke Skywalker was attacked by a wampa who dragged him back to its cave. Some quick thinking helped Luke avoid being the wampa's next meal.

1

WAKE UP
Luke regained consciousness and found himself stuck inside a wampa's cave. He was hanging upside down from his feet and was far, far away from any help!

2

CONCENTRATE
Luke's lightsaber was lying a few feet away from him. He concentrated and used the Force to pull the weapon toward him.

3

BREAK FREE
Luke used his lightsaber to cut himself free, just as the wampa rushed toward him.

4

THINK
The Jedi was intimidated by the wampa's monstrous size, but he had to act quickly in order to avoid being eaten!

5

ATTACK!
While the wampa tried to swipe at Luke with its large claws, Luke chopped off the monster's arm with his lightsaber. Luke made his escape as the wampa cried out in pain.

On Tatooine, a herd of banthas in the distance is nothing to be scared of. A bantha ridden by a Tusken Raider, however, is a fearful sight for every moisture farmer and Jawa as raiders ride banthas when they attack! Adult banthas are large and strong. They grow up to 2.5 meters (8 feet 2 inches) tall and are extremely heavy. A Tusken Raider riding a bantha is almost unstoppable.

When the astromech droid R2-D2 ran away on Tatooine, young Luke Skywalker and his droid C-3PO went to look for him. Along the way, Luke saw a group of Tusken Raiders and their banthas. When Luke stopped to watch, one of the raiders surprised and attacked him, and Luke was nearly killed. Fortunately, clever Obi-Wan Kenobi scared the attacker away by making sounds like a krayt dragon.

The krayt dragon of the Dune Sea is one of the few natural enemies of banthas and the largest predator on Tatooine. The giant dragon is rarely seen, as it sleeps buried in the sand during the day. Once, C-3PO came across the bones of a krayt dragon lying on the dunes after it died. The skeleton was enormous and stretched up to 30 meters (98 feet)!

Monsters as Pets

Despite being wild and at times looking scary, some monsters can actually make great pets. With a bit of careful training, they can be surprisingly helpful and even entertaining!

Dog-like massiffs make excellent security guards and will attack intruders. These ferocious creatures are a favorite of Tusken Raiders on Tatooine.

Rock worrts and womp rats can be handy to keep around the home because they will eat pests. Once in a while though, monsters are kept as pets simply because they are beautiful or just very funny.

Some monsters may look cute when they are small, such as baby rancors or wampas, but when they grow up, they become too dangerous to keep as pets. If they get loose they may even attack and eat their owners!

The best place to buy a pet is the planet Coruscant, where legal traders and illegal smugglers sell monsters of all shapes and sizes. Senators on Coruscant like to keep pets, but they are not the only ones. Even crime lords, pirates, and gangsters such as Jabba the Hutt keep little monsters as sidekicks.

Some of Jabba the Hutt's pets were very helpful. Bubo was a frog-dog that Jabba kept as a guard. This monster was an ugly little creature, feared more because of his looks than the harm he could cause. He dragged his fat stomach between his two short legs and had a large mouth of long, spiny teeth. His bulging eyes oozed as if he had a bad cold, and drool ran down his wide chin. Frog-dogs are not as dumb as they may seem—they are actually very intelligent little monsters. In fact, when an assassin named Ree-Yees tried to kill Jabba, Bubo swallowed a bomb detonator in order to foil the deadly plot and save his gangster boss.

Jabba the Hutt also kept worrts in and around his palace to eat pests. Worrts look a lot like frog-dogs, but these amphibians have two very long arms as well as two short legs. They have spines for protection on their backs, and two sensitive antennae on their heads, which help them detect approaching enemies and prey.

Worrts will try to eat anything that moves, including womp rats, nunas, gorgs, and ibians. They shoot their long, sticky tongues out to catch food. But sometimes they miss, and end up swallowing stones.

Some pets are kept just because they are fun to have around, such as Salacious Crumb. This monkey-lizard from the planet Kowak snuck onto Jabba's ship and was caught stealing his food. Normally Jabba would have killed anyone stealing from him, but he found the monkey-lizard amusing, so he decided to keep the creature as a pet.

Monkey-lizards are very clever and can copy the speech of other beings. They love teasing those around them. Salacious Crumb once pulled one of C-3PO's eyes out when the droid was working as Jabba's slave!

Massiffs are large reptiles that live on Geonosis and Tatooine. Their tough, leathery skin is covered in scales and armor plating, while stiff black spines run down their backs. They have excellent eyesight, and can smell with both their nose and tongue.

In the wild, massiffs hunt in packs and attack their prey with sharp claws and fangs. Massiffs are good to have around though because they will eat annoying pests. They are often kept as camp guards by Tusken Raiders and they are used to guard the tunnels and arena on the planet Geonosis.

RANCOR

Monster, captured by Jabba

Scary
- Terrified victims swallowed whole

Not so scary
- Not naturally dangerous
- Attacks when abused or hungry

SCARY METER

WHO IS THE
SCARIEST?

WAMPA

Hoth snow beast

Scary
- Vicious hunter
- No mercy or regrets

Not so scary
- Wampa babies are cute
- Sleeps a lot

SCARY METER

GREEDO

Bounty hunter for Jabba

Scary
- Will destroy anyone or do anything if the price is right

Not so scary
- Not very smart and only dangerous if paid

SCARY METER

SPACE SLUG

Solitary space monster

Scary
• Will eat anything, including a small asteroid or a starship

Not so scary
• Mindless being, will eat whatever it can find

SCARY METER

Some creatures look very strange and even quite scary. Appearances, however, can be deceptive. Sometimes the most bizarre characters are actually very intelligent and even quite likeable. Other times they are even worse than they appear and will try to eat you.

ACKLAY

Combat monster in arenas

Scary
• Terrifying, blood-thirsty killer

Not so scary
• Needs to kill and eat meat to survive

SCARY METER

EPHANT MON

Jabba's chief of security

Scary
• Looks repulsive

Not so scary
• Intelligent being, hard worker, and a loyal friend

SCARY METER

While some pets make good guards or are kept for amusement, others are useful for transportation. On the planet Utapau, the local Utai and Pau'an population raise giant feathered lizards called varactyls to ride around their sinkhole cities.

Varactyls are friendly and intelligent monsters with very good memories. A varactyl named Boga came in handy when Jedi Obi-Wan Kenobi was chasing General Grievous on the planet Utapau.

These gentle monsters look like giant lizards, and have a beaked face surrounded by a mane of feathers. Their 10 meters (33 feet) long tail is covered in long feathers, which helps them keep their balance when climbing steep walls. Varactyls eat only plants so they are easy to take care of.

Obi-Wan observed that like most varactyls, Boga was obedient and brave. Boga continued to carry Obi-Wan on her back even when they were being fired upon!

VARACTYL CHASE

Jedi Obi-Wan Kenobi is in trouble. He has been sent to Utapau to defeat the Separatist cyborg, General Grievous. The general is a threatening sight—is he too much for the Jedi?

1

VICIOUS FACE-OFF
General Grievous fights with four lightsabers at once, but that does not scare Obi-Wan Kenobi. The Jedi defeats Grievous after a long battle.

2

VARACTYL STEED
Grievous realizes he cannot win the lightsaber duel and escapes on his wheel bike. Obi-Wan calls hi varactyl steed, Boga, and chases Grievous

3

THE CHASE
Obi-Wan drops his lightsaber during the bumpy ride, but does not give up the chase. The Jedi grabs Grievous's deadly electrostaff and attacks him.

4

VICTORY
Obi-Wan is knocked over the edge of a cliff during the duel. He uses the Force to grab a blaster lying close by, shoots at Grievous, and destroys him.

Space Monsters

Monsters can thrive in the most unlikely environments.

It is hardly surprising then that some monsters can even survive among the stars and asteroids in space. These creatures do not need oxygen to live and they can grow to be very big.

In space, food of any kind is limited. Monsters must adapt to feed on whatever resources are available, including asteroids, starships, energy from suns, and, of course, other monsters lurking in space.

Spaceports can be dangerous places because monsters hitch rides in cargo ships that dock there. Monsters that hide on starships are transported around the galaxy—unless they eat the entire starship along the way! Finding a monster on a ship while traveling in deep space can be terrifying, so it is important to do regular checks for stowaways.

Sometimes when space monsters are accidentally transported from one planet to another they become more than just an irritating pest. In the worst cases, these alien species can wipe out the local wildlife on an unsuspecting world.

The smuggler Han Solo and his faithful Wookiee companion, Chewbacca, piloted a starship called the *Millennium Falcon*. They encountered some very unusual monsters during their many adventures in the galaxy.

Han Solo once flew the *Millennium Falcon* into what seemed to be a cave on an asteroid, while dodging the evil Imperial fleet. Soon he and his friends discovered they had actually flown into the belly of a gigantic space slug!

Space slugs are found all over the galaxy. These creatures normally grow to be 10 meters (33 feet) long, but in the asteroid fields around the planet Hoth, they can grow up to 900 meters (2,953 feet) long, and can swallow a whole starship! Han Solo managed to fly out of the slug's belly, just as it began to close its mouth and swallow the *Falcon*!

Space slugs use their long tails to dig tunnels into asteroids and live inside them. They get most of their nutrients from the minerals inside asteroids, but will gladly eat

anything that flies into or near their tunnels. They use their large, sharp teeth to capture prey and keep them from escaping. Smaller slugs eat and digest winged, bat-like creatures called mynocks. Sometimes the mynocks survive in the bellies of larger space slugs and live as parasites.

Mynocks manage to survive in space by attaching themselves to starships and eating the power cables and energy conductors. If they are not cleared from the ship quickly, they can drain all the energy and leave the passengers stranded in space.

When mynocks are swallowed by a giant space slug, they can live inside the slug's belly and share its meals. They may also nibble on the unfortunate slug from the inside, too. The slug is so huge that the mynocks do little harm.

Mynocks have large wings covered in a thin layer of skin, which makes them look like giant bats. Mynocks may look scary, but humans actually have nothing to fear from them. A mynock will not attack a human, but droids like C-3PO make a great snack!

While inside the space slug, the *Millennium Falcon* was attacked by a group of mynocks. Chewbacca had to shoot them with his powerful bowcaster weapon to get them off the ship. Han Solo also got rid of a mynock with his blaster, before he discovered they were all inside the slug together.

Space monsters are even more dangerous when they are inside rather than outside a starship. A snake-like dianoga lived inside the trash compactor of a huge starship called the Death Star. Once, when Luke Skywalker got trapped in the trash compactor, the

dianoga wrapped its long tentacles around Luke and nearly drowned him! Fortunately, dianogas are cautious monsters. It got scared when the trash compactor was turned on, making loud noises, and it let Luke go.

Dianogas are originally from the muddy planet Vodran, but they are found on many other planets, too. Because they thrive in the dirtiest conditions, they can be found living in the garbage tanks and sewers of every spaceport.

When they are small, dianogas can be quite useful. They search for pests in the sewers of cities like Coruscant with their large, single green eye. When they find duracrete worms, granite slugs, or mutant rats they reach out with their long tentacles and drag them underwater, tearing them apart with their hidden fangs.

MONSTER
FOOD CHAINS

Monsters are not that fussy about what they eat. While some may occasionally devour a Jedi, they mostly prey on each other. It's a monster-eat-monster world!

SEA FOOD
The sando sits at the top of Naboo's food chain. The colo and the opee must always watch out for the sando, or else they may become its next meal.

SANDO

FROZEN FOOD
On planet Hoth, wampas will happily eat a rebel soldier, a stormtrooper, or a Jedi if they can catch one. But most of the time, they will dine on tauntauns.

WAMPA

FAST FOOD
In the wild, rancors like to eat large herbivores, but in captivity they will eat anything—sometimes even their Gamorrean guards.

RANCOR

COLO AND OPEE

TAUNTAUN

GAMORREAN
GUARD

Winged Beasts

The monsters of the air are just as diverse as the beasts of the sea and land. In the skies of planets across the galaxy there are flying insects, reptiles, mammals, and other creatures that are harder to describe. Some monsters are found on only one planet. Others have been brought to different worlds as pets, or working beasts, or even by accident.

Most flying monsters live on worlds with land, but some live on water-covered planets such as Kamino, where they had to evolve in order to swim and fly.

Winged beasts were especially important during the Clone Wars. Jedi Knights and members of the Republic rode them through the skies in battles against the droid armies. Flying monsters don't need expensive fuel. They also blend in with the natural environment and understand local dangers. In contrast, the droid army used flying machines, which struggled to cope in the harsh weather conditions, such as high winds and rain, of the planet. On Utapau, the native population rode on gigantic dactillions when they battled against enemy droids.

When the climate of Kamino became warmer, the ice caps melted, flooding the planet and destroying much of the native life there. The Kaminoans developed cloning technology and engineered themselves and other life forms to adapt to the new watery environment. They also brought "flying whales," called aiwha, from Naboo to Kamino, and bred them to suit the watery planet. Kaminoans use the aiwha to travel between their floating cities.

Aiwhas are gentle creatures and live in small family groups, or pods. They feed by both filtering water of the Kaminoan seas for tiny creatures and catching larger fish with their teeth.

Aiwhas are very similar to the flying thrantas on Bespin. Aiwhas have broad wings and a long tail that allows them to swim in the sea and fly very long distances. When swimming, these flying monsters pull their two wings to their side and thrash their tail, launching high into the sky.

Can-cells are giant flying insects that
use four wings instead of two. These monsters
are native to the Wookiee homeworld of
Kashyyyk. Wookiees keep can-cells as pets
and have even designed their ornithopter
ships to fly like them. The insects are
attracted to the familiar sounds and flight
patterns of the ships and follow them into
battle. These green-eyed creatures were an
important part of the aerial fleet belonging
to the Wookiee army. Can-cells were also
the perfect size for small Jedi Masters to ride
during the Battle of Kashyyyk.

Dactillions are flying reptiles from the planet Utapau. These meat-eaters once preyed upon terrified Utapauns as well as their varactyl pets. The Utapauns discovered, however, that dactillions could be tamed if they were fed red meat. The Utapauns raise them from eggs and ride them across their sinkhole cities and up to the planet surface. Dactillions were used in battles against General Grievous and his droid armies during the Clone Wars.

Arena Beasts

Execution arenas are popular in the Outer Rim worlds, especially on the dry, desert planet of Geonosis. Prisoners are brought into a large, dusty arena and made to fight fierce and bloodthirsty creatures in front of large crowds, who have gathered to watch the prisoners battle for their lives.

Gangsters such as Jabba the Hutt bet on the outcomes of deadly matches between these prisoners and the terrible monsters. The arena monsters are among the most

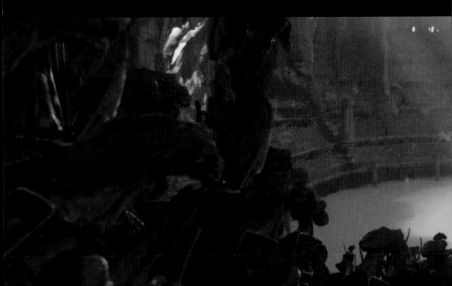

brutal beasts in the galaxy. They are often rare and valuable species who are chosen for their aggressive and vicious nature. Usually brightly colored, the large beasts are easily seen by the crowds even from their seats high up in the arena. Like the prisoners forced to fight them, arena monsters are also kept captive. They are treated badly in order to make them ferocious.

The Petranaki arena on the planet Geonosis is infamous for organizing some of the most gruesome arena fights in the whole of the galaxy.

THE GEONOSIS
ARENA TOUR

Petranaki arena on Geonosis was built out of a natural rock formation and can seat thousands of spectators. Crowds flock to witness the execution of prisoners, who are made to fight some of the galaxy's most ferocious monsters.

Anakin riding a Force-controlled reek, surrounded by deadly droidekas.

Reek pen, with food stores to the side.

Pit of carnivorous worms being starved for future spectacle.

Upper ledges with bird's-eye view taken only by latecomers.

High-ranking officials sit under membrane awnings at the arena.

Soldier droids in sentry houses watch out for surface predators.

An acklay attacking Jedi Obi-Wan Kenobi.

Execution pillars

A picador encouraging a monster to attack prisoners in the arena.

The most frightening and formidable arena monster is the acklay, from the jungle planet of Vendaxa. Acklays are popular monsters for executions on Geonosis because of their gruesome hunting habits.

On their home planet, acklays prefer to live underwater. They emerge during the day to hunt reptiles called lemnai. Walking on their six long claw-like legs, they stab the lemnai with their bony claw-tips. Acklays wave their legs in the air like swords, and slice their prey in half. Then they use their

powerful jaws and sharp dagger-like teeth to tear through the lemnai's shell.

Jedi Obi-Wan Kenobi faced a ferocious acklay when he was sentenced to death at the Petranaki arena on Geonosis. The acklay tried to stab Obi-Wan with its claws, but accidently smashed the chains that tied the Jedi to a pillar. Obi-Wan managed to free himself and get hold of a lightsaber. With his trusty weapon restored, he cut off the acklay's claws and destroyed the beast.

ARENA BEAST
The bloodthirsty crowd went wild when the acklay entered the Petranaki arena. Famous for its slashing attacks, the acklay made a deadly opponent.

Obi-Wan's Padawan, Anakin Skywalker, and Senator Padmé Amidala were also captured and sent into the Petranaki arena on Geonosis. Anakin was attacked by another powerful creature known as a reek.

Reeks are herbivores, which come from the moss-covered Codian Moon. In the wild, they live in herds and eat wood moss. However, Geonosians discovered that if they

starved the reeks, they would become aggressive and eat meat. This horrible treatment made them perfect arena beasts.

Reeks have tough red and brown skin, covered in scaly bumps. When charging at an opponent, its horns are its deadliest weapons. Their teeth are also made of horn and continue to grow throughout their lives. They are so tough that they are able to bite limbs off of opponents.

Anakin used his Jedi powers to control the charging reek. Once he calmed it down, he rode it across the arena and saved his friends.

The cat-like nexu is from the forests of the planet Cholganna, but it has been smuggled into the arenas of Geonosis. Nexu have very good eyesight and a secondary pair of eyes to sense the body heat of nearby prey. They are good climbers and hunt high in the trees, catching tree-dwelling creatures.

Nexu are well-adapted to forest life. Thick, sleek fur keeps them warm during forest nights, while the stripes on their coat provide camouflage and help them sneak

up on prey. Sharp, deadly quills on their
backs protect nexu from predators
attacking from above.

    Padmé was attacked by
a nexu in the arena. She
climbed on top of a pillar
to escape. The vicious beast
tried to climb up, too, and
almost reached her. Luckily,
Anakin's reek charged at
the nexu and stopped it.

A DAY IN THE LIFE OF A
GEONOSIAN PICADOR

Insect-like Geonosian drones work hard as picadors in the Petranaki arena. The picadors spend their days goading beasts and taunting prisoners, and they do it happily!

1 **RISE AND SHINE**

Picadors sleep together inside the grooves of a hive, waking up at first light to begin their duties. They don't have any privacy in the hive so they enjoy going to work.

GEONOSIAN PICADOR

Geonosian drones have been genetically modified for a variety of additional roles, such as service, labor, soldier, farmer, and overseer drones. Picadors are one of the few honored positions to which a drone can aspire.

TEND TO ORRAY

Orrays have a mind of their own. Riding them every day keeps the orrays trained in the arena, and helps keep their mind off what they would rather do: eat Geonosian eggs!

3 TIE UP PRISONERS

Picadors bring the prisoners into the arena and tie them to large columns. They must tether them securely. If prisoners get away, the monsters might attack the picadors instead!

PUT ON A GOOD SHOW

The picadors must keep the monsters interested, but not let them destroy prisoners too quickly. It is their responsibility to deliver the most entertaining performance.

Monsters as Weapons

In the wrong hands, monsters can become deadly weapons. Gangsters and criminals across the galaxy make many enemies, thanks to all their cheating, stealing, and double-dealing. One of the most dangerous criminals, Jabba the Hutt, devised some creative ways of getting rid of his rivals. The twisted Hutt often used rare monsters as executioners!

Jabba had many business connections, so he was able to locate and smuggle into his palace the most exotic monsters in the galaxy. Yet one of his favorite monsters lived close by: a bizarre creature known as the sarlacc. Jabba enjoyed ordering his enemies to be fed to the sarlacc. He even traveled to the Dune Sea on his sail barge just to watch!

Another favorite of Jabba the Hutt was a fierce beast called a rancor. He received it as a birthday present and kept it imprisoned underneath his palace.

Rancors are very rare, but have become famous across the galaxy for their strength. Adult rancors can grow to an intimidating 5 meters (15 feet 5 inches) tall! Their enormous claws and razor-sharp teeth make them powerful opponents. They are well protected by the natural armor plates on their backs and shoulders—not even blaster fire can penetrate that tough armor.

Contrary to their reputation, rancors are not naturally aggressive and live a solitary life. Females carry a pair of offspring on their backs or stomachs for three years. Poachers often steal the babies and sell them to gangsters. On several worlds, rancors are kept as pets, or are trained to carry heavy goods and used as battle mounts. A rancor can, however, become quite ferocious if it is abused and starved. Such was the case for the rancor belonging to Jabba the Hutt.

If Jabba was angry with someone in his court, he would drop them into the rancor pit. This is what happened to Jedi Luke Skywalker. With Luke's skills and quick thinking, however, he managed to destroy the monster.

TOUR OF THE
RANCOR PIT

The ferocious rancor lives in a hidden pit beneath Jabba the Hutt's palace. A trapdoor in Jabba's throne room opens to drop a hapless victim straight into the path of the hungry monster.

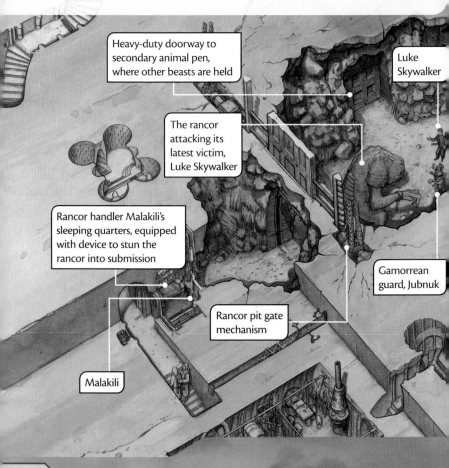

Heavy-duty doorway to secondary animal pen, where other beasts are held

Luke Skywalker

The rancor attacking its latest victim, Luke Skywalker

Rancor handler Malakili's sleeping quarters, equipped with device to stun the rancor into submission

Gamorrean guard, Jubnuk

Rancor pit gate mechanism

Malakili

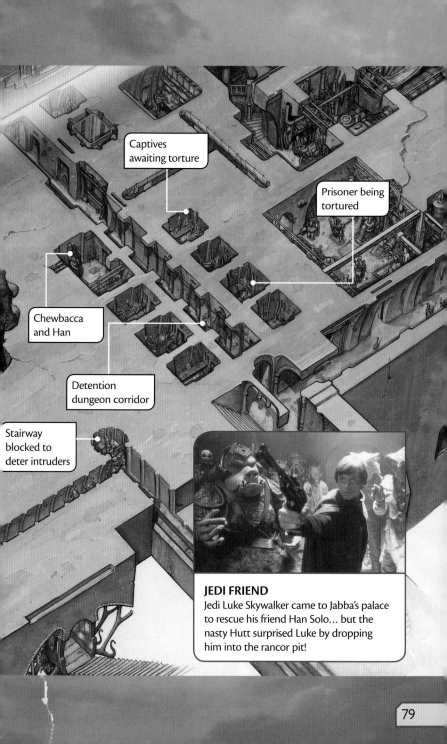

Captives
awaiting torture

Prisoner being
tortured

Chewbacca
and Han

Detention
dungeon corridor

Stairway
blocked to
deter intruders

JEDI FRIEND
Jedi Luke Skywalker came to Jabba's palace
to rescue his friend Han Solo... but the
nasty Hutt surprised Luke by dropping
him into the rancor pit!

WHO HIRED WHOM?

Villains across the galaxy prefer to get monsters to do their dirty work. Sith Lords, criminals, and gangsters alike believe a monster will do the job well. But there are times when it seems to go all wrong.

COUNT DOOKU
This Sith Lord hired bounty hunter Jango Fett and Poggle the Lesser to carry out assassination missions on his behalf.

JANGO FETT
The notorious Jango Fett often hired other bounty hunters to complete his dangerous missions.

JABBA THE HUTT
Gangster Jabba the Hutt needed to eliminate many enemies. He enjoyed using unusual monsters, such as sarlaccs and rancors to dispose of them.

MALAKILI
This monster handler may have worked for Jabba, but his real loyalty was to the Hutt's rancor, which he loved dearly.

POGGLE THE LESSER

Poggle was the Archduke of Geonosis. On Count Dooku's command, he sentenced Obi-Wan, Anakin, and Padmé to death by monsters in the Petranaki arena.

ARENA MONSTERS

Poggle's acklay was relentless because it was so hungry. Eventually Obi-Wan Kenobi destroyed it with his lightsaber.

ZAM WESELL

Jango Fett hired bounty hunter Zam Wesell to assassinate Padmé Amidala, using kouhuns.

KOUHUNS

Kouhuns are silent and deadly. Fortunately for Senator Padmé, Jedi Anakin Skywalker destroyed the kouhuns before they poisoned her.

THE RANCOR

Jabba's rancor was supposed to eat Luke Skywalker, but when it was unexpectedly destroyed by the Jedi, it broke Malakili's heart.

THE SARLACC

Jabba liked to feed his enemies to the sarlacc, but in the end it actually ate a lot of the Hutt's friends and henchmen.

The mighty sarlacc is a nightmarish, tentacled monster, though, fortunately, it is very rare. The most infamous sarlacc is nested in the Pit of Carkoon in the Dune Sea on Tatooine. Jabba liked to feed his unlucky prisoners to this sarlacc. Luke Skywalker and his friends faced this horrible fate and survived only thanks to the quick-witted Jedi who had hidden a lightsaber inside R2-D2.

From above, only a sarlacc's mouth is visible. The rest of the creature, including a vast stomach covered in roots and eight long limbs, are buried deep in the sand. When a victim is pushed into the pit, the sarlacc's tentacles grab them and drag them into its mouth. Hundreds of spear-like teeth prevent the victim from climbing out. The sarlacc squeals as its beaked tongue forces a meal into its belly, swallowing the victim whole!

The bounty hunter Boba Fett is the only person known to have escaped from the bowels of a monstrous, hungry sarlacc.

THE SARLACC

Few monsters in the galaxy are as famous, as feared, or as mysterious as the mighty sarlacc. The best-known sarlacc lives in the desert on Tatooine. Not much is known about sarlaccs, as most scientists agree that this monster is far too dangerous to study.

MALE OR FEMALE?

Only adult female sarlaccs can be seen from above ground. Tiny males live as parasites, attached to females in the sand far below. Baby sarlaccs crawl to the surface and wander as nomads for several years until they find a home.

Beaked tongue

Upper
stabilizing limb

Boba Fett trying
to escape

BURIED BEAST

Only the mouth of a
sarlacc is visible from above.
The rest of its enormous
body, stomach, and legs are
buried underground, where the
sarlacc digests its victims
for a thousand years.

DATA FILE
Width: 3 m (9 ft 10 in)
Strengths: tentacles,
many rows of teeth,
beaked tongue
Weaknesses: adults can't
run away, susceptible
to blaster fire

Parasitic
male

C-3PO

Han
Solo

"Oh, dear. His High Exaltedness, the great Jabba the Hutt, has decreed that you are to be terminated immediately."

"Good, I hate long waits."

 "You will therefore be taken to the Dune Sea and cast into the Pit of Carkoon, the nesting place of the all-powerful sarlacc."

"Doesn't sound so bad."

 "In his belly, you will find a new definition of pain and suffering, as you are slowly digested over a thousand years."

"On second thoughts, let's pass on that, huh?"

Creepy Crawlies

The creepy crawlies of the galaxy range from annoying to deadly. Some sting or bite, while other species carry diseases. They can destroy ships, make whole towns sick, and in extreme cases wipe out many lives. But they all have a part to play—even if just to be food for other creatures.

Creepy crawlies look for dark places to hide where temperatures are cool, and they have easy access to food and water.

Unfortunately, their favorite hiding places include areas where people live. This makes some of these creatures a very frightening matter for their neighbors. Creepy crawlies such as duracrete slugs, conduit worms, and kouhuns may be found inside the home of a moisture farmer on the dry, desert planet of Tatooine, or in the dark halls of Jabba's palace. Annoying pests are always trying to invade the towering insect hives where the Geonosians live. Such little monsters can become big trouble, especially among the streets and towering buildings of the Republic's capital planet, Coruscant.

Many creepy creatures lurk in Coruscant's underworld. Conduit worms feed on electrical fields surrounding power wires in cities, computers, and even large starships. They have no heads, tails, or brains and can grow new body parts as needed. This amazing ability allows conduit worms to infect millions of miles of electrical wiring.

Citizens of Coruscant's underworld fear power blackouts as that is when conduit worms come out to look for new sources of energy. The worms can sense electrical activity in brains and will try to wiggle their way inside people's heads through their ears, mouth, or nose while they sleep!

Duracrete slugs are often accidentally transported to worlds like Coruscant by passing cargo ships. These slugs eat stones and the foundations of buildings, causing great damage to Coruscant's lower levels.

Normally, duracrete slugs grow three to five meters (nine to 16 feet) in length, but on Coruscant, some are over 10 meters (33 feet) long. The slugs are almost blind and so they feel their way around using tentacles on their mouths. As they crawl along they produce a layer of toxic slime that helps them move across surfaces easily while they feed.

Sometimes special circumstances call for a creepy crawly to be brought in from a faraway planet. The dangerous bounty hunter Jango Fett had a sinister plan to do away with Senator Padmé Amidala on Coruscant. There had already been many unsuccessful attempts on her life, but Jango was convinced that the poisonous, centipede-like kouhuns from the planet Indoumodo would succeed in the mission where other methods had failed.

Kouhuns are fast and silent, which makes them perfect for assassination plots! They have long, white bodies with 29 pairs of legs, long feelers on their heads, and a stinger on their tails. Poison in their stinger can paralyze a victim, while the venom in their bite can be fatal.

Jango hired Zam Wesell, another bounty hunter, to deliver the monster assassins to Padmé's apartment while she was asleep. Zam and Jango had starved the kouhuns, making them hungry so that they might hunt down Padmé more quickly.

The creatures sensed Padmé's body heat with their feelers and crawled to her bed. The assassination attempt was thwarted when Padmé's Jedi friend Anakin Skywalker sensed danger and burst into her room, slicing the kouhuns in two with his lightsaber.

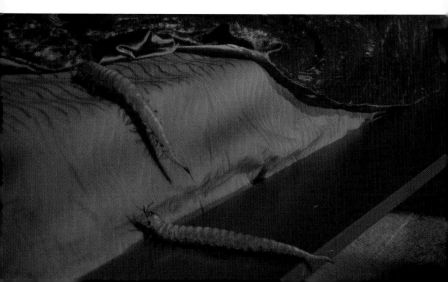

NARROW ESCAPE
The small, yet very venomous, kouhun was about to sting Padmé while she slept. Luckily, Anakin Skywalker arrived just in time.

There are plenty of horrible pests on
the planet Tatooine. Rock warts are orange
creatures with eight legs and four eyes.
They hide in dark, rocky areas where they
wait for prey. They are very poisonous—one
bite can kill a person in moments.

Rock warts are wild creatures, but
sometimes they sneak inside Jabba's palace to
get out of the hot sun. Normally they don't
attack large animals, but if they are

frightened or stepped on, they will react with a painful and deadly bite.

As a young boy, Luke Skywalker encountered other creepy monsters on Tatooine— womp rats. These nasty rodents live in garbage heaps around dusty towns like Mos Eisley, arriving in large packs and spreading diseases.

Luke used his experience of destroying womp rats in his T-16 airspeeder to help him later in battle. He once told his pilot friend Wedge Antilles that shooting a small target on a massive spacecraft was just as easy as shooting womp rats on Tatooine.

FANGS AND CLAWS

Sharp fangs, pointy claws, bone-crushing horns—these are just some of the features monsters use to attack enemies, capture prey, and defend themselves.

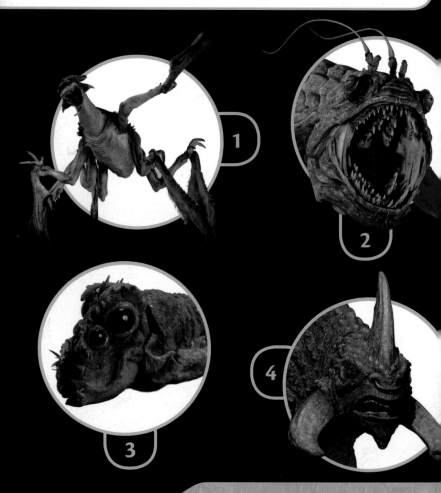

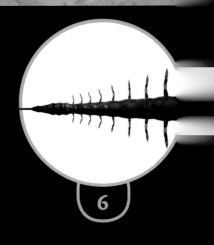

KEY

1. ACKLAY
Long claws for stabbing prey.

2. OPEE SEA KILLER
Sharp teeth for trapping prey.

3. ROCK WART
Mouth venom for
poisoning enemies.

4. REEK
Big horns for charging at
and stabbing opponents.

5. NEXU
Sharp claws for cutting open
prey, and for climbing.

6. KOUHUN
Stinger tail for injecting
venom into its prey.

7. COLO CLAW FISH
Face claws for grabbing prey.

8. SARLACC
Beaked tongue for swallowing
victims whole.

Working Monsters

Some monsters can be trained to carry riders, weapons, or heavy supplies for their masters. They must be strong and obedient, and able to walk long distances for their jobs. Rebel Alliance soldiers, Jedi, clone troopers, stormtroopers, and bounty hunters all ride monsters from time to time. Local populations such as those of Naboo often use seemingly monstrous creatures for official ceremonies and events.

The droid armies of the Trade Federation and Separatists never use monsters, as they do not value any living things. They rely on machines instead.

Working monsters need to have different abilities on each planet. On Naboo, the monsters must be able to swim and walk through murky swamps and tall grasslands. Creatures on Hoth must survive the freezing cold and be able to walk well in deep snow. Pack animals on Tatooine must work in the extreme heat with very little water. On Felucia, beasts must be good climbers and have protection from the sun's harmful rays. On other planets, monsters may need to jump far or even fly. Working monsters are well-adapted to survive in their own environment.

The Gungans of Naboo used many different monsters as war beasts in their battle against enemy droid armies. Giant fambaas transported shields that protected the entire Gungan army. Falumpasets pulled battle wagons full of blue energy-ball bombs to the front line. Kaadus carried soldiers onto the battlefield.

Kaadus may look funny because of the strange way they walk, swaying from side to side, but their two long legs help them run swiftly through any terrain. They are also good swimmers and can stay underwater for a very long time. Fambaas are one of the largest types of monster on Naboo. They lay their eggs in the water and their babies are born with gills and a tail, so they look like giant tadpoles. Baby fambaas look adorable with their fat tummies and stumpy little legs. But as adults they have hard, dry lizard-like skin and can grow up to 15 meters (49 feet) tall!

Falumpasets have long legs, which are helpful for walking through the Naboo grasslands. They can swim, but can't hold their breath underwater for very long. During official ceremonies, the falumpaset is used as a mount for the Gungan leader Boss Nass.

GUNGAN GRAND ARMY
The Gungan army stood fearlessly under
a protective energy bubble while facing
off droid soldiers of the Separatist army.
The bubble shield was generated by
machines carried on the backs of fambaas.

GUNGAN ARMY AND WEAPONS

The Gungan army uses monsters in creative ways along with powerful weapons to make them a formidable force on the battlefield. Tanks and flying ships better watch out!

Kaadu adorned with feathers for battle

KAADU

Kaadus never slow down while charging at the enemy. This makes these agile beasts perfect for Gungans to ride on and attack foes in battle.

Saddlehorn used for steering

Hoof-like claws help kaadu move swiftly

Waterproof skin

FAMBAA SHIELD GENERATORS

In battle, Gungans create a bubble-like defensive shield around themselves by using two fambaas that work together as a team. Each carries a different machine.

SHIELD PROJECTOR DRUM

The fambaa at the rear carries a drum that receives energy from the fambaa in front. The energy bounces off the drum, creating a shield bubble.

Shield projecto drum

Energy distribut

Long legs for crossing grasslands

FALUMPASETS
Battle wagons are pulled by hardy falumpasets. The wagons carry supplies and energy-ball bombs.

WAR TOOLS
Gungan weapons are powered by blue plasma. Catapults and hand-held devices launch destructive energy balls.

Whistle

Energy ball

Energy shield _Atlatl_ _Cesta_

SHIELD ENERGY EMITTER
The fambaa in front carries the shield energy emitter. A Gungan soldier rides this fambaa and shoots energy toward the drum mounted on the fambaa behind him. The safety of the entire Gungan army depends on this one soldier.

Electrically isolated operator cockpit

Shield energy emitter

Overload discharge prongs

Bridle harness reinforces obedience

Tauntauns are the most common monsters found on the icy world of Hoth. They are very well adapted to the extremely cold temperatures of this planet.

Tauntauns are covered in scales like a reptile: thick fur hanging over these scales protects them from cold winds. They have two sets of nostrils that take turns breathing, which warms the air coming through their nose and into their bodies very efficiently.

Rebel Alliance soldiers on Hoth prefer to use tauntauns for scouting missions, as their vehicles do not work well in snowstorms. Han Solo and Luke Skywalker also rode tauntauns on Hoth. On one particular mission, Luke's beast was killed by a hungry wampa and Han's tauntaun died in the extreme

cold. Han used Luke's lightsaber to cut a
hole in his dead tauntaun so Luke could
rest inside where it was warm and survive
the freezing temperatures. It smelled terrible,
but Luke survived!

SNOW CREATURE

The furry tauntaun is one of the few beings that can survive the cold, at least during the day, on the planet Hoth. Rebel soldiers trained these beasts to carry riders over great distances.

On the desert world of Tatooine, dewbacks, eopies, and rontos are popular working monsters. They are used for a variety of jobs, such as carrying loads or transporting people.

Most of the time these monsters are used for good, but sometimes they are also used for evil. When Princess Leia sent R2-D2 on a mission to find

Obi-Wan Kenobi on Tatooine, Darth Vader sent stormtroopers to look for the droid and his friend, C-3PO. Sandstorms on Tatooine can easily damage Imperial speeder bikes, so the stormtroopers chose to ride dewbacks instead.

Dewbacks are hardy beasts, which walk slowly to avoid wasting too much energy and water. But, if they have to, they can run for short distances. These large reptiles are called dewbacks because each morning they lick the dew off each other's backs. Tatooine is a very dry planet so this is one of the few ways they can find water.

Eopies are the hardest-working beasts on Tatooine. They are comfortable to ride and can pull heavy loads. Jedi Qui-Gon Jinn used an eopie to drag a heavy hyperdrive generator across the desert after Queen Padmé Amidala's starship was attacked and damaged by the Separatist army.

Eopies have long necks with extended, flexible snouts. This makes it easy for them to pick and eat prickly desert plants. The gentle eopies do not have any natural defenses and can escape only by outrunning their predators or spitting at them. They sometimes fall into sarlacc pits, too, from where they cannot escape.

Rontos are large, strong reptiles that can pull huge machines. They make good pack animals and are loyal to their masters. Desert scavengers, known as Jawas, use them to carry supplies and droid parts from the Mos Eisley space port.

These monsters have excellent hearing because of their two sets of different-sized ears. Their large ears hear low sounds and their small ears listen for high-pitched noises. They cannot see very well though, and often get startled by sudden movements. A scared ronto can accidentally knock its Jawa rider and all his supplies off its back!

During the Clone Wars on the planet
of Felucia, the Republic clone troopers rode
a strange monster called a gelagrub.

It is very difficult to travel in Felucia,
especially with a speeder bike, walker, or
tank. Thick forests of fungus grow everywhere

and get in the way. This makes riding gelagrubs the best way to travel. These large, blue-green grubs have many legs that allow them to climb around or even on top of the fungus. Their two round eyes sit one above the other on top of their heads, which helps them spot predators from above, such as rancors or droid ships.

Gelagrubs have to eat all the time, not just for energy, but also because they are constantly growing and changing. The gelagrubs are actually baby monsters. They are the larvae of giant Felucian ground beetles. After they grow nearly 4 meters (13 feet) long, they change into even bigger monsters with a hard, black shell.

WHEN MONSTERS ATTACK...

**NEXU
VS.
PADMÉ**

**MYNOCK
VS.
HAN SOLO**

**ACKLAY
VS.
OBI-WAN**

When Padmé Amidala faced a vicious nexu in an arena, she climbed on top of a pole out of its reach. The nexu was eventually destroyed by a reek.

Mynocks are pesky, fast, and hide deep inside ships where they can eat the wiring. A sharp-shooting Han Solo blasted them when they attacked the *Millennium Falcon*.

Acklays are deadly. However, a skilled Jedi like Obi-Wan Kenobi was able to fend one off with a Geonosian picador's long spike, keeping the beast at arm's length.

The bigger the monster, the harder it is to defeat. Monsters don't always need to be destroyed in order for them to be outmatched, but sometimes heroes must think quickly to escape alive!

MONKEY-LIZARD
VS.
R2-D2

REEK
VS.
ANAKIN

RANCOR
VS.
LUKE

When Jabba's pet Salacious Crumb attacked C-3PO and took his eye out, R2-D2 zapped the monkey-lizard with a bolt of electricity and saved C-3PO.

Reeks are stubborn and very strong. Padawan Anakin Skywalker used the Force to control a ferocious reek in the Petranaki arena on Geonosis.

Sometimes thinking fast and being resourceful can save lives. Jedi Luke Skywalker wedged a bone in a rancor's mouth to prevent it from eating him.

MONSTER
RECORDS

The galaxy is home to many bizarre creatures of all shapes and sizes. They include some real record breakers. From the most venomous to the heaviest and the longest, find out which monster is number one!

LONGEST

1. Conduit worm (Unlimited)
2. Giant space slug
(900 meters; 2,953 feet)
3. Sando aqua monster
(160 meters; 525 feet)

STRONGEST

1. Fambaa (4,900 kg; 10,802 lbs)
2. Rancor (3,225 kg; 7,110 lbs)
3. Reek (1,975 kg; 4,354 lbs)

1. Varactyl (330 kph; 205 mph)
2. Tauntaun (85 kph; 53 mph)
3. Kaadu (61 kph; 38 mph)

VENOMOUS

**1. Rock wart (can kill a creature
as large as 21 men)**
2. Kouhun (can kill a creature as
large as 17 men)
3. Colo claw fish (can paralyze only)

LONGEST-LIVING

HEAVIEST

**1. Giant space slug (201,175 kg;
443,515 lbs)**
2. Sando aqua monster (48,987 kg;
107,997 lbs)
3. Sarlacc (22,588 kg; 49,799 lbs)

1. Sarlacc (50,000 years)
2. Giant space slug
(45,000 years)
3. Greater krayt dragon
(10,000 years)

Quiz

1. Where does the colo claw fish hide while waiting for its prey?

2. The bones that C-3PO found on Tatooine belonged to which monster?

3. Are Ephant Mon or Greedo monsters?

4. Which planet do wampas live on?

5. How many pairs of legs does a kouhun have?

6. Whose eyes does the monkey-lizard Salacious Crumb pull out?

7. What kind of a monster is Bubo?

8. What length can the space slugs around the planet Hoth grow up to?

9. Which monster lived on the Death Star?

10. Aiwhas live in which two environments?

11. Who is attacked by a nexu in the
    Petranaki arena?

12. What do acklays eat
    on their home planet?

13. Who takes care of
    the rancor belonging to Jabba the Hutt?

14. How long do sarlaccs live?

15. Which Gungan monsters carry
    shield generators?

See page 127 for answers

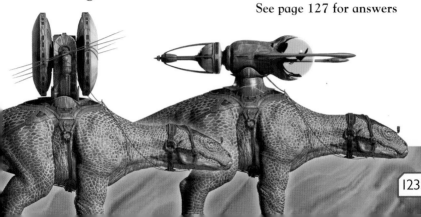

Glossary

Abyss
A deep hole that seems endless.

Amphibian
A cold-blooded animal with smooth skin that lives in and around water, such as frog-dogs.

Antennae
A long stalk, usually on an animal's head, which helps it to feel or listen.

Arena
A large area for public entertainment.

Assassin
A person who destroys an important person, sometimes in return for payment.

Asteroid
Rocks floating in space.

Bounty Hunter
Someone who captures or destroys a wanted person in return for payment.

Camouflage
Something blending into the background so that it becomes difficult to see.

Death Star
Moon-sized battle station, with a laser that can destroy entire planets.

Environment
The surrounding natural world, including plants, animals, rocks, water, and air.

Executioner
Someone (or something) whose job it is to destroy a prisoner.

Ferocious
Something fierce, violent, and dangerous.

Geonosians
Intelligent insect-like beings who live in hive cities on the planet Geonosis.

Gungans
Intelligent creatures who live in underwater cities on the planet Naboo.

Herbivores
Creatures who eat plants and not meat.

Jedi
A group of beings who defend peace and justice in the galaxy.

Jawas
Small creatures who wear hooded robes and live on the planet Tatooine.

Larva
The early stage of life for insects and amphibians, before they change into adults.

Luminescent
Something that gives off light.

Mammal
A warm-blooded animal with hair or fur that feeds its babies on the mother's milk.

Moisture Farmers
Settlers on Tatooine who use machines to collect water from the air.

Paralyze
To prevent something from being able to move.

Parasite
A harmful creature that must live in or on another animal to survive.

Plankton
Tiny creatures that drift in the sea or fresh water.

Predator
An animal that hunts other animals to eat them.

Prey
An animal that another creature catches to eat.

Reptiles
Cold-blooded animals with dry, scaly skin, such as massiffs, dactillions, or lemnais.

Savage
Something violent and wild with no self-control.

Sinkhole
Deep, wide hole on a planet's surface, such as those on the planet Utapau.

Sith
Enemies of the Jedi who use the dark side of the Force.

Smugglers
Someone who buys, sells, or transports items illegally.

Species
A group of similar animals that can mate and make babies.

Tribubble Bongo Submarine
Ships built by Gungans to travel underwater in the Naboo seas.

Tusken Raider
Desert-dwellers from Tatooine who are very hostile to outsiders.

Vacuum
A place that is completely empty, with no land, water, or air, such as in space.

Venom
Poisonous liquid that an animal injects with its teeth or stinger.

Wookiee
A shaggy, tree-dwelling species from Kashyyyk.

Index

Quiz answers
1. In limestone caves 2. The krayt dragon 3. No, Ephant Mon and Greedo
are intelligent beings. 4. Hoth 5. 29 6. C-3PO's eyes 7. A frog-dog
8. 1,000 meters (3,280 feet) 9. A dianoga 10. Air and sea 11. Padmé Amidala
12. Lemnais 13. Malakili 14. 50,000 years 15. Fambaas

Like this book? Try another DK Adventure!

Star Wars®: Sith Wars
Meet the Sith Lords who are trying to take over the galaxy. Discover their evil plans and deadly armies.

Star Wars®: Jedi Battles
Join the Jedi on their epic adventures and exciting battles. Meet brave Jedi Knights who fight for justice across the galaxy.

Terrors of the Deep
Marine biologists Dom and Jake take their deep-sea submersible down into the world's deepest, darkest ocean trench, the Mariana Trench.

In the Shadow of the Volcano
Volcanologist Rosa Carelli and her son Carlo are caught up in the dramatic events unfolding as Mount Vesuvius re-awakens.

Clash of the Gladiators
Travel back in time to ancient Rome when Gladiators entertained the crowds—will they be spared death?

Galactic Mission
Year 2098: planet Earth is dying. Five school children embark on a life or death mission to the distant star system of Alpha Centauri to find a new home.

Twister: A Terrifying Tale of Superstorms
Jeremy joins his cousins in Tornado Alley for the holidays. To his surprise, he discovers they are storm chasers and has the ride of his life.